Illinois from A to Z

Betty Carlson Kay

Illinois

from

A *to* Z

University of Illinois Press
Urbana and Chicago

Publication of this book was supported
by a grant from Joan and James J. Stukel.

Library of Congress Cataloging-in-Publication Data
Kay, Betty Carlson
Illinois from A to Z / Betty Carlson Kay.
p.   cm.
Includes bibliographical references.
ISBN 0-252-02540-7 (alk. paper)
1. Illinois—History—Miscellanea. 2. Illinois—Biography—
Miscellanea. I. Title
F541.6.K39   2000
977.3—dc21   99-050497

C 5 4 3 2 1

To my husband, John, for generous love
and to my daughter, Margret, for her "Just do it!" style

Illinois from A to Z

A

Jane Addams

Thousands of immigrants moved to Chicago in the late 1800s, bringing with them their own languages, customs, and beliefs. Some of them felt overwhelmed by the big city, just as many newcomers do today.

Jane Addams saw the need for a settlement house where immigrants could get help, education, and child care. The founder of Hull-House also fought for child labor laws, women's right to vote, and world peace. In 1931 she received the Nobel Peace Prize.

Today, the original Hull-House is a

museum. The Hull-House Association carries on the tradition of "neighbors helping neighbors" with programs that address current problems such as drug abuse and domestic violence as well as recurring problems of child care and housing assistance.

B

Bituminous Coal

Millions of years ago, Illinois was covered by swamps. When the tall ferns and treelike plants in the swamps died, layers of peat were formed. The weight of rocks and sand on top of the peat compressed it into bituminous coal, a black rock that can be burned to produce energy and heat.

Illinois has the largest reported bituminous coal resources in the United States. Coal lies beneath 65 percent of the state and is dug out by deep mining and surface methods. It is used widely and is the best kind of coal because it can be crushed easily.

The proud tradition of coal mining in Illinois faces challenges in the twenty-first century. Miners must work in safe conditions; clean air standards must be met; and mined land must be returned to its original appearance. Meeting these demands will allow the industry to mine coal to produce energy for our power-dependent society.

C

Chicago

The first permanent settler in Chicago was Jean Baptiste Point du Sable, a black fur trader who came up from New Orleans in 1779 to establish a trading post on the Chicago River. From these meager roots, Chicago mushroomed in the 1800s to become the city of the century. Although Mrs. O'Leary's cow wasn't responsible for the Great Fire on October 8, 1871, that burned down much of Chicago, the catastrophe did provide an opportunity for the city to rebuild itself in a safer, more orderly fashion.

While Chicago's reputation for political corruption and gangsters during the Roaring Twenties has never been completely forgotten, such nicknames as "The City of Big Shoulders" and "The City That Works" point to the true character of its residents. Chicago is also called "The Second City," even though it's now the *third* largest city in the United States.

Among the many things Chicago is famous for are its skyscrapers and neighborhood bungalows, deep dish pizza and elegant restaurants, jazz bands and the Chicago Symphony Orchestra, windy walks over the Michigan Avenue bridge and hot summer afternoons on miles of Lake Michigan beaches.

D

John Deere

In 1837, a blacksmith from Grand Detour, Illinois, named John Deere had a great idea for keeping the clay in prairie soil from sticking to the iron plows that farmers used. He took an old circular saw blade and forged it into a smooth steel plow blade.

His invention was so successful that he moved to Moline in 1847 and started his own company. Incorporated in 1868, that company is now the leading farm equipment manufacturer in the world. It also makes construction and lawn care equipment.

Another man with a great idea also helped to change the way farmers worked the land. His name was Cyrus McCormick, and he arrived in Chicago at the age of 38 with $60 in his pocket, a patent for a reaper, and lots of determination.

Cyrus McCormick saw the need for mechanical reapers to cut the acres of wheat as the wide prairies opened up to settlers. By 1856 his fledgling company was making 15 reapers a day.

Today, reapers have been replaced with combines, which not only cut the grain but process it too. Cyrus McCormick's reaper company is now part of the Case Corporation in East Moline, Illinois, where both combines and cotton pickers are made.

E

Exposition

The 1893 World's Columbian Exposition celebrated the 400th anniversary of Christopher Columbus's arrival in the Americas. It also showcased Chicago's accomplishments. Buildings were erected, streets were flooded to resemble canals, and more electricity than was used throughout the rest of Chicago helped to illuminate "The City of Light." Proud residents were so boastful that Chicago picked up another nickname, "The Windy City."

One of the highlights of the Exposition was an enormous wheel built in Galesburg, Illinois, by George W. Ferris. The Ferris wheel was supported by two 140-foot steel towers and had 36 bus-sized wooden cars that held 60 people each. The wheel was also used at the 1904 St. Louis Exhibition before being scrapped in 1906.

The Eli Bridge Company, founded in 1900 in Jacksonville, Illinois, is the oldest maker of Ferris wheels in continuous operation.

F

Enrico Fermi

An Italian scientist named Enrico Fermi experimented for almost 10 years before finding a way to split open an atom and use the powerful force that holds its nucleus together. After he won the Nobel Prize for Physics in 1938, he moved to the United States.

In 1942 at the University of Chicago, a team of scientists led by Enrico Fermi achieved the first nuclear chain reaction. One result of their success was the development of nuclear bombs, whose devastating power was used to end World War II.

During the period known as the cold war, many countries threatened world peace by manufacturing and stockpiling nuclear weapons. Today, most countries concentrate on peaceful uses of nuclear energy, such as the production of electrical power. In addition, nuclear magnetic resonance has become a powerful diagnostic tool in the fields of medicine and health care.

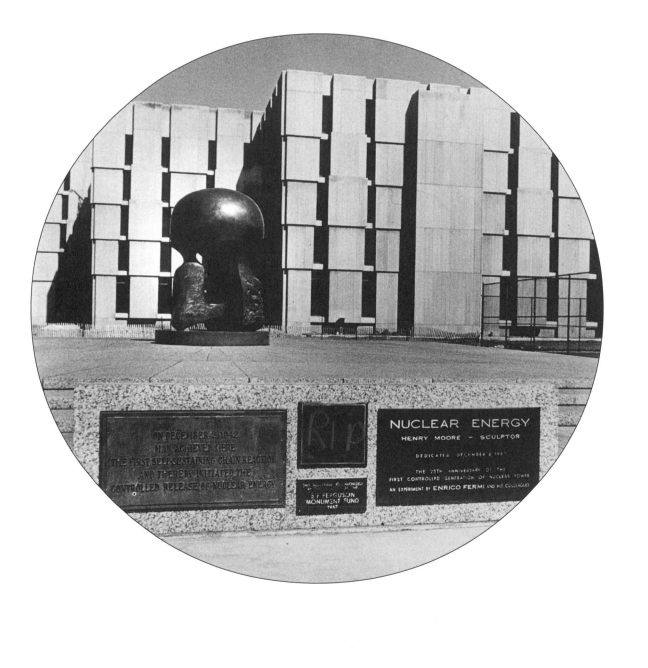

Ulysses S. Grant

Known for his energy and determina-
tion, Ulysses S. Grant commanded the
victorious Union Army at the close of
the Civil War. After the Confederate
Army surrendered at the Appomattox
Court House, this man of compassion
released General Robert E. Lee and his

soldiers on their honor and allowed them to keep their horses "for the Spring plowing."

Upon his return to Galena, Illinois, after the Civil War, General Grant was given a home, which is now a state memorial. In 1869 a grateful nation elected him president of the United States. He served two terms and tried to bring the North and South together again.

In 1881, after traveling in Europe and the Far East, the former president settled in New York City and, with Mark Twain as his publisher, wrote his memoirs. He and his wife are both buried in Grant's Tomb in New York City.

H

Haymarket Riot

In the late 1880s, which was a time of great labor unrest, a combination of long hours, low pay, and unhealthy working conditions led Chicago-area workers from slaughterhouses, meat-packing plants, and factories to try to form unions. A peaceful rally at

Haymarket Square in 1886 was just winding down when the police arrived and an unknown person tossed a bomb into the crowd, killing several policemen and civilians.

Eight labor leaders, six of whom were not even at the rally and two who were on the speaker's wagon, were arrested for what Henry D. Lloyd reported was "the violent insanity of their public speeches." After an unfair trial, four of the men were hanged, one committed suicide, and three were sentenced to life in prison. In 1893 Governor John Altgelt, who was a friend of labor, essentially ended his political career when he freed the three men.

Labor Day, which we celebrate on the first Monday in September, has roots in the Haymarket riot. At the base of the monument to the Haymarket martyrs in Forest Park are these words: "The day will come when our silence will be more powerful than the voices you are throttling today."

I

Illiniwek

Twelve small tribes of Native Americans banded together for protection and support and gave themselves a big name, Illiniwek, which means "The Men." Our state is named after the Illinwek, or Illini Indians.

The Illiniwek were a migratory people. In the summer they lived along the riverbanks in large rectangular lodges. In the winter they divided into smaller groups and lived in wigwams. These dome-shaped houses were covered with bark or with mats woven from cattails.

In 1673 there were 10,000 Illiniwek in the central Mississippi River Valley. Father Jacques Marquette, a French missionary, wrote in 1674 that "they live by hunting, game being plentiful in that country, and on Indian corn, of which they always have a good crop; consequently, they have never suffered from famine."

By 1832, when they surrendered the last of their Illinois land to the United States government, there were only 300 Illiniwek left in one small village. Today their descendants are represented by the Peoria Indian Tribe of Oklahoma, which has about 2,650 members.

Jolliet and Marquette Visit Great Village of Illinois, August 1673 (painting by Robert A. Thom)

J

Louis Jolliet

While trading for beaver pelts in French Canada, the explorer, map-maker, and fur trader Louis Jolliet was told about a big river to the south that flowed to the sea. Hoping to discover a trade route to the Far East, he set out in 1673 with Father Jacques Marquette, a French missionary who spoke several Native American languages, to explore the Mississippi River. But they turned around when they realized that they were heading toward the Gulf of Mexico, not west to the Pacific Ocean.

On their way back to Canada,

Louis Jolliet and Father Marquette took a shortcut up the Illinois River, portaging across to the Chicago River. It would be 175 years before the Illinois and Michigan Canal linked these rivers and opened up trade and travel between the Great Lakes and the Gulf of Mexico.

One of the last steam-powered boats on the I&M Canal, the Margaret *hauled wood between Channahon and Joliet, Illinois.*

K

Ray Kroc

A man named Ray Kroc who lived in Oak Park, Illinois, sold milkshake mixing machines. When the owners of a restaurant in San Bernadino, California, bought quite a few of his machines, he just had to ask, "Why do you need so many?" Dick and Mac McDonald explained that they ran their restaurant like an assembly line and had to prepare a lot of food very quickly. Ray Kroc liked the idea of fast service and good food and became a franchise agent for the McDonald brothers.

April 15, 1955, was opening day for the first McDonald's restaurant in Des Plaines, Illinois. In 1961 Ray Kroc bought out the McDonald brothers and continued the now-famous Golden Arches™ tradition.

By 2000 there were more than 26,000 McDonald's restaurants in 119 countries around the world. Hamburger University™ in Oak Brook, Illinois, offers McDonald's employees a "bachelor of hamburger-ology" degree.

McDonald's #1 Store Museum, Des Plaines, Illinois

L

Abraham Lincoln

In the early 1800s, long before he became the sixteenth president of the United States and signed the Emancipation Proclamation, Abraham Lincoln lived the life of a typical settler on the Illinois prairie, perhaps harder than some but surely easier than others.

So what makes him a man we admire, even revere?

Certainly, his honesty, hard work, love of learning, and compassion are important elements. So too are his years of riding the Eighth Judicial Circuit as a friendly young lawyer, an experience that served "Honest Abe" well when he sought elective office.

Abraham Lincoln is also recognized for his "way with words," from his powerful Gettysburg Address to such homespun reflections as these:

"Resolve to be honest at all events; and if in your own judgment you can not be an honest lawyer, resolve to be honest without being a lawyer" (July 1, 1850).

"Stand with anybody that stands right. Stand with him while he is right, and part with him when he goes wrong" (October 16, 1854).

The Birdman Tablet

M

Mounds

About 1,000 years ago, a thriving population of Native Americans built hundreds of earthen mounds in what we now call Illinois. Platform mounds held residences, storehouses, and temples. Conical mounds probably were burial sites.

Ridge-top mounds were defense markers.

Members of this Mississippian culture grew corn, hunted, and traded with other Indians. To help keep track of time, and probably to set planting dates, they put poles in the ground, lining them up with the sun in a circular fashion—a cedar "Woodhenge."

These Indians believed in a natural order to the universe and tried to balance their lives within it. The Birdman Tablet, unearthed in 1971, depicts the Upper World (the falcon's beak) and This World (the warrior) on the front;

the Lower World is represented on the back by a snakeskin pattern.

Over time the Indians were driven from the area. Many of the mounds were explored and looted. Others were plowed under so that crops could be planted. Many more of the mounds were leveled during highway construction. Thanks to archaeological preservation efforts, about 80 of these mounds survive and tell us a great deal about the remarkable people who built them.

New Salem

Thanks to a gristmill and sawmill on the Sangamon River, New Salem was a prosperous trading center and home to about 25 families between 1829 and 1837. A young man named Abraham Lincoln began his adult life there, and when he left, according to Benjamin P. Thomas, he carried with him "a conviction of the essential worth and right-mindedness of ordinary people."

Although the town itself failed, its pioneer spirit lived on. Interest in restoring New Salem was boosted by the newspaper magnate William Randolph

Hearst in 1906 when he bought 62 acres containing the site of the town and gave it to the Old Salem Chautauqua Association. In 1919 the state of Illinois took over, and in 1932 a complete restoration was begun. Today, volunteers re-create the lively town as tourists enjoy a window into the past.

Orphan Trains

ASYLUM CHILDREN!

A Company of Children, mostly Boys, from the New York Juvenile Asylum, will arrive in

ROCKFORD, at the Hotel Holland,

THURSDAY MORNING, SEPT. 6, 1888,

And Remain Until Evening. They are from 7 to 15 Years of age.

Homes are wanted for these children with farmers, where they will receive kind treatment and enjoy fair advantages. They have been in the asylum from one to two years, and have received instruction and training preparatory to a term of apprenticeship, and being mostly of respectable parentage, they are desirable children and worthy of good homes.

They may be taken at first upon trial for four weeks, and afterwards, if all parties are satisfied, under indentures,—girls until 18, and boys until 21 years of age.

The indenture provides for four months schooling each year, until the child has advanced through compound interest, and at the expiration of the term of apprenticeship, two new suits of clothes, and the payment to the girls of fifty, and to the boys of one hundred and fifty dollars.

All expenses for transportation will be assumed by the Asylum, and the children will be placed on trial and indentured free of charge.

Those who desire to take children on trial are requested to meet them at the hotel at the time above specified.

E. WRIGHT, Agent.

PLEASE EXTEND THIS INFORMATION.

In 1842 the New York Association for the Improvement of the Conditions of the Poor began "placing out" the city's poor, homeless children. Believing that healthier living conditions could be found on farms in the Midwest, thousands of children boarded "orphan trains" bound for small towns in Illinois and other states.

At prearranged stops the children were lined up so adults could make their selections. Those who weren't chosen got back on the trains and rode to the next stop. Some children were chosen by people who wanted little more than to be loving parents. Unfortunately, many more were chosen just to be farmhands.

The orphan trains ran until 1929. Between 100,000 and 200,000 children came to live in the Midwest in this way.

P

Poets

Gwendolyn Brooks, the poet laureate of Illinois, grew up in a part of Chicago called "Bronzeville." She named her first book of poems *A Street in Bronzeville.* Her second book, *Annie Allen,* won a Pulitzer Prize in 1950.

Here is part of a poem by Brooks called "Narcissa":

Small Narcissa sits upon
A brick in her back yard
And looks at tiger-lilies,
And shakes her pigtails hard.

Gwendolyn Brooks

Vachel Lindsay is a poet who lived in Springfield, Illinois, but loved to walk out in the country, talking with folks and listening to the sounds of the world. His poems

Vachel Lindsay

feature strong rhythms and vivid images.

Here is part of Lindsay's poem "The Little Turtle," which is still enjoyed by many schoolchildren:

He snapped at a mosquito.
He snapped at a flea.
He snapped at a minnow.
And he snapped at me.

&

Carl Sandburg lived in Galesburg, Illinois, and wanted to be the voice of the American people. He won two Pulitzer Prizes, one in 1940 for his biography *Abraham Lincoln: The War Years* and one in 1950 for poetry.

One of Sandburg's Chicago poems is called "Fog":

The fog comes
on little cat feet.

It sits looking
over harbor and city
on silent haunches
and then moves on.

Carl Sandburg

Quilts

More than warmth, comfort, and love, quilts are a link to the past and to the future. An inherited quilt may be a reminder of a childhood visit to a distant relative, or the fabric scraps used in the quilt may have come from clothing worn by a loved one. Sewing a quilt today recalls past quilting bees, when neighbors gathered around the quilting frame and envisioned future generations yet to snuggle in the memories being made.

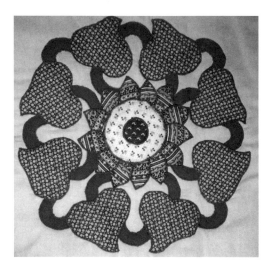

The Illinois Quilt Research Project recognized that quilts are valuable, fragile pieces of history and began documenting them in 1986. More than 15,800 quilts were registered by the project. Some were old, some were new, but all of them had a story to tell. Each one of them has an Illinois connection.

Leah Thornburgh of Havana, Illinois, completed the blocks and border for this "Jackson Star" quilt in 1849. Her great-granddaughter, Alice M. Smith, finished the quilt in 1990.

R

River

Many thousands of years ago, after the glaciers had finally receded from the Upper Midwest, a small river was left flowing eastward into a big lake. The area became the perfect place first for Native Americans and then for fur traders and settlers to live.

Around 1855, the rapidly expanding city of Chicago built a sewer system that relieved a number of sanitary problems but created an even bigger one. It seems that the sewers drained into the east-flowing Chicago River, which emptied into Lake Michigan, which is where the city got its drinking water!

The best solution to the problem was to reverse the flow of the river. The shallow Illinois and Michigan Canal was dredged, and in 1871 the river began flowing in the opposite direction. But the solution proved only temporary, until the deep-cut Sanitary and Ship Canal was completed in 1900. It had taken millions of dollars, thousands of mostly immigrant laborers, and many years to make the reversal permanent.

In 1955, in recognition of the ingenuity and technical skill involved, the American Society of Civil Engineers named the Chicago Sanitary and Ship Canal one of the Seven Wonders of American Engineering.

Summit Lock #1, Chicago, 1870

S

Springfield

Abraham Lincoln and eight other legislators, who were called the "Long Nine" because of their height, successfully lobbied to have Springfield named our state capital in 1839. Thanks to our sixteenth president's political fame, Springfield is now a destination for tourists from around the world.

Everyone knows that rubbing the nose on the bronze bust at the entrance to Lincoln's tomb in the Oak Ridge Cemetery brings you good luck. But it also means that there's a very shiny nose on a very big statue!

The Old State Capitol, completed in 1841, has been beautifully restored and is open to the public. Beneath the building are facilities used by the Illinois State Historical Library. The new capitol building, completed in 1888, is where the work of the state continues.

T

Team Sports

Several professional sports teams call Chicago their home. Near the lakefront is Soldier Field, where the Chicago Bears football team plays.

The Chicago Cubs, of the National League, play baseball in the "friendly confines" of Wrigley Field, where "bleacher bums" bask in the sun just beyond the famous ivy-covered outfield wall and many fans watch the games from the rooftops of nearby buildings.

The White Sox, of baseball's American League, are building new traditions at their new Comiskey Park, which is on the city's South Side.

The Chicago Bulls, who renewed the city's interest in professional basketball in the 1990s and won an incredible six NBA championships, play in the new United Center on the Near West Side.

The Chicago Blackhawks, of the National Hockey League, also call the United Center their home. Because the hockey and basketball seasons overlap, when the Blackhawks are in town the wooden basketball floor and a layer of felt are removed to reveal an icy playing surface. No wonder Bulls fans with courtside seats are chilly even when the games heat up!

U

Underground Railroad

The famous passageway from slavery to freedom sometimes operated underground in tunnels and cellars and sometimes used railcars, but it was never literally a railroad under the ground. Instead, kind-hearted people, both black and white, fed and sheltered runaway slaves in barns, caves, and secret hiding places before sending them on to the next "station."

Two Illinois brothers were especially outspoken in their views against slavery. Elijah Lovejoy published the anti-slavery newspaper *The Alton Observer* and was killed in 1837 while defending his presses. Owen Lovejoy was a preacher who hid runaway slaves behind a fake wall in his attic, the opening concealed by a chest of drawers. He declared: "Owen Lovejoy lives at Princeton, Illinois, . . . and he aids every fugitive that comes to his door."

With the passage of the 13th Amendment in 1865, the work of the underground railroad was completed. But the struggle for equality continues to this day.

$50 Reward!!!

RANAWAY from the subscriber, living in Tipton county, Tennessee, a negro man slave, named

HARRY,

about 24 years of age, 5 feet 11 inches high, very stout built, with large fore teeth and very wide spaces between them, rather slow of speech, but speaks distinct and clear; had on when he left, a blue cassinet coat, and blue home-spun janes pantaloons; he went away on the 10th of May last, and is expected to steer to St. Clair county, Illinois, where he has a mother living.

Whoever will apprehend and confine said slave, so that the owner gets him again, and give information to George Evans, at Jonesborough, Union county, Illinois, shall receive the above reward, and all lawful charges.

OWEN EVANS.

July 13, 1833.

14-4t*

V

Voting Rights

In **1818** Illinois became a state, but only "white male inhabitants above the age of 21 years" could vote.

In **1870** the 15th Amendment to the U.S. Constitution declared that voting rights could not be denied (to males) due to race, color, or prior servitude.

In **1873** Illinois women were able to hold school offices, but they were not allowed to vote in these or any elections.

In **1891** the Illinois General Assembly granted women the right to vote in school board elections only.

In **1913** Illinois became the first state east of the Mississippi River to grant women the right to vote for the president and for local officials—but they had to use separate ballots and ballot boxes!

In **1919** Illinois was the first state to ratify the 19th Amendment, which gave women in all states the right to vote.

Today, all eligible voters are encouraged to register and then to vote in local, state, and national elections. Learning about issues is the surest way to increase voter participation in the electoral process of our democracy.

Frank Lloyd Wright

In 1887 a young architect named Frank Lloyd Wright moved to Chicago, a city of opportunity that was still rebuilding after the Great Fire of 1871. He made famous the Prairie style of architecture, which included long horizontal roof lines to mirror the flat, expansive prairie and large living areas that seemed to flow into each other.

The Dana-Thomas House in Springfield, Illinois, is probably the best preserved and most complete of Wright's Prairie style houses. He is also known for designing furniture, stained glass, gardens, and even linens to achieve harmony inside and outside the home.

Wright's own home and office, as well as many examples of his special style of architecture, can be seen in Oak Park, Illinois.

Detail from the living room of the Dana-Thomas House

The Dana-Thomas House

X

Exchange

During the last half of the 1800s, its centralized location, extensive railroad connections, and vast stockyards made Chicago a clearinghouse for much of the nation's grain and livestock.

Buying and selling on South Water Street, where huge quantities of grain overflowed the warehouses, was a confusing exchange of money for bags of wheat until the idea of exchanging warehouse receipts took hold. Next came the desire to lock in prices and delivery dates before the grain was even harvested, which led to buying and selling "futures" on the commodities markets.

Today, traders at the Chicago Mercantile Exchange, where cattle and hog futures are traded, and at the Chicago Board of Trade, which handles grain futures, treasury notes, and bonds, use a method called "open outcry" to exchange goods: they stand in the pits, give hand signals, and shout out their buy and sell orders to other traders.

Although the amount of grain and livestock shipped to The Windy City is now quite small, farmers, those who purchase their goods, and investors all closely follow the Chicago commodities markets.

Y
Yield

Thousands of years ago, after the waters that covered what is now Illinois had receded and after the Ice Age had flattened the land, buffalo roamed freely on the prairie, where the grass grew as tall as an adult man or woman.

This "sea of grass" flourished in the hot summers and cold winters of Illinois. Underneath the prairie grass was fertile, black soil that was prized by the farmers who came with plows strong enough to cut through the tangled roots. Soon, farms replaced much of the prairie.

Today, the bounty from Illinois farms helps to feed the world. In order to get the maximum yield from their crops of corn and soybeans, farmers use modern machinery and computers. A global positioning system, or GPS, helps them to locate their exact position in the field and then calculate the amount of seed and fertilizer needed for the best results in each area. Farmers realize that how they treat the land today will affect their yields for many years to come.

Z

Zoos

The Lincoln Park Zoo in Chicago is the oldest zoo in the United States, courtesy of a pair of swans that were a gift from the commissioners of Central Park in New York City and were first displayed to the public in 1868. Soon visitors to the zoo could also see buffalo, peacocks, deer, wolves, and eagles.

In 1949 the Lincoln Park Zoo gained national attention thanks to its director, Marlin Perkins, who hosted a live weekly television series called "Zoo Parade." In recent years, the zoo has emphasized making the exhibits more like the natural homes of animals in the wild. Best of all, admission is still free.

Brookfield Zoo, also in Chicago, is known for its naturalistic, multispecies exhibits, such as Habitat Africa and Tropic World. In Tropic World, which is one of the largest indoor zoo exhibits anywhere, visitors walk on a pathway that overlooks pools and waterfalls and makes it easy to see a wide variety of animals and vegetation. Rain and thunderstorms occur in this humid rainforest, but because of the height of the pathway, only the animals get wet!

Recommended Reading

For Children

Bial, Ray. *Corn Belt Harvest.* Boston: Houghton Mifflin, 1991.

———. *Frontier Home.* Boston: Houghton Mifflin, 1993.

———. *The Underground Railroad.* Boston: Houghton Mifflin, 1995.

———. *Where Lincoln Walked.* New York: Walker and Co., 1997.

———. *With Needle and Thread.* Boston: Houghton Mifflin, 1996.

Brooks, Gwendolyn. *Bronzeville Boys and Girls.* New York: Harper and Row, 1956.

Cugnet-Bannatyne, Jo. *A Prairie Alphabet.* Quebec: Tundra Books, 1992.

Freedman, Russell. *Lincoln: A Photobiography.* Boston: Clarion Books, 1987.

Fritz, Jean. *Just a Few Words, Mr. Lincoln.* New York: Grossett and Dunlap, 1993.

Fry, Annette R. *The Orphan Trains.* New York: Macmillan, 1994.

The Living Museum 60, no. 1 (Spring/Summer 1998). Published by the Illinois State Museum, Springfield.

Murphy, Jim. *The Great Fire.* New York: Scholastic Books, 1995.

"Placing Out." *Cobblestone Magazine* 19, no. 4 (April 1998): 13–17.

Shemie, Bonnie. *Mounds of Earth and Shell.* Quebec: Tundra Books, 1993.

Wood, Marion. *The World of Native Americans.* New York: Peter Bedrick Books, 1997.

For Adults

Elbert, E. Duane, and Rachel Kamm. *History from the Heart: Quilt Paths across Illinois.* Nashville: Rutledge Hill Press, 1993.

Miller, Donald L. *City of the Century.* New York: Simon and Schuster, 1997.

Illustration Credits

Jane Addams   Both photographs (negs. 613, 839) are by Wallace Kirkland, courtesy of the Jane Addams Memorial Collection, University Library, University of Illinois at Chicago.

Bitiminous Coal   Background and aerial photographs courtesy of the Illinois Coal Association.

Chicago   Detail of the water tower and waterworks after the fire of 1871 courtesy of the Chicago Historical Society (ICHi-02792, photographer unknown). Chicago skyline seen from atop the Ferris wheel at Navy Pier courtesy of the author.

John Deere   "His First Lesson" courtesy of Deere and Company. Detail from an early plowing scene and the McCormick reaper courtesy of the Illinois State Historical Library.

Exposition   All three photographs courtesy of the Illinois State Historical Library.

Enrico Fermi   Enrico Fermi at the blackboard and *Nuclear Energy* (Henry Moore sculpture) at

the University of Chicago courtesy of the University of Chicago Library.

Ulysses S. Grant   Both photographs courtesy of the Illinois State Historical Library.

Haymarket Riot   Both photographs courtesy of the Illinois State Historical Library.

Illiniwek   Photograph of Robert Thom's painting courtesy of the Illinois State Historical Library.

Louis Jolliet   Engraving of Louis Jolliet courtesy of the Illinois State Historical Library. Steam-powered boat on the I&M Canal courtesy of Robert E. Sterling, Joliet, Illinois.

Ray Kroc   Ray Kroc with a Multimixer in the background and McDonald's #1 Store Museum, Des Plaines, Illinois, both used by permission of McDonald's Corporation.

Abraham Lincoln   Both photographs courtesy of the Illinois State Historical Library.

Mounds Birdman Tablet (photograph by Peter Bostrom) and aerial view of Cahokia Mounds, c. 1150 A.D. (painting by William R. Iseminger), courtesy of the Cahokia Mounds State Historic Site.

New Salem Both photographs courtesy of the Illinois State Historical Library.

Orphan Trains Announcement courtesy of the Illinois State Historical Library. The orphan train, c. 1900s, courtesy of the Kansas State Historical Society, Topeka (Santa Fe Collection, box 40, 55/21.148).

Poets All photographs courtesy of the Illinois State Historical Library.

Quilts Quilt detail courtesy of the author. "Jackson Star" quilt courtesy of the owner, Alice M. Smith, and the Early American Museum, Mahomet, Illinois.

River A tributary of the Fox River at Moraine Hills State Park, courtesy of Jason Lindsey, Perceptive Visions. Summit Lock #1, Chicago, 1870, courtesy of the Illinois State Historical Library (NG-8715).

Springfield Lincoln bust courtesy of the author. Old State Capitol courtesy of the Illinois State Historical Library.

Team Sports Michael Jordan statue courtesy of the author. Wrigley Field, Chicago, c. 1965, courtesy of the Chicago Historical Society (ICHi-24457, photographer unknown).

Underground Railroad Reward poster courtesy of the Illinois State Historical Libary. Dresser in Lovejoy's home courtesy of Raymond Bial.

Voting Rights Suffragette float, Chicago, July 4, 1910, courtesy of the Chicago Historical Society (ICHi-20157, photographer Charles R. Clark).

Frank Lloyd Wright Frank Lloyd Wright, courtesy of the Frank Lloyd Wright Archives, Scottsdale, Arizona. Detail from the living room (#10-22, photographer Pedro Guerrero) and exterior view of the Dana-Thomas House (DH.89.F.13.1, photographer Doug Carr) courtesy of Frank Lloyd Wright's Dana-Thomas House State Historic Site, Springfield, Illinois.

Exchange Entrance to Union Stockyards, c. 1910, courtesy of the Chicago Historical Society (ICHi-19107). Trading pit courtesy of the Communications Department, Chicago Board of Trade.

Yield Corn detail courtesy of Copenhaver Cumpston. Cultivating soybeans courtesy of Jim Foster. GPS graphic courtesy of Guido Strotheide.

Zoos Tropic World at the Brookfield Zoo courtesy of the Chicago Zoological Society (photographer Jim Schulz). Lincoln Park Zoo courtesy of the author.

Memoriam The Eastland Disaster, Chicago, 1915, courtesy of the Chicago Historical Society (*Chicago Daily News* photographer).

Acknowledgments

The author sincerely thanks the following people for their input, interest, and support:

Thomas F. Schwartz, Illinois State Historian

Illinois State Historical Library staff, especially Kathryn Harris, Mary Michals, Robert Salata, and Kim Bauer, Curator of the Henry Horner Lincoln Collection

Taylor Pensoneau, Illinois Coal Association, and Ernest Ashby, Illinois Department of Natural Resources ("Bituminous Coal")

Matthew Cook, Rights and Reproductions Coordinator, Chicago Historical Society ("Chicago" and "Teamwork")

Jim Doyle, Project Manager in the Trademark Group, and Leslie Stegh, Archivist, John Deere Corporation ("John Deere")

Dr. Mike Wiant, Curator of Anthropology, and Nina Walthall, Assistant Curator of Education, Illinois State Museum ("Illiniwek")

Customer Satisfaction Department, McDonald's Corporation, Oak Brook, Illinois ("Ray Kroc")

Nancy Sherbert, Kansas State Historical Society ("Orphan Trains")

Cheryl Kennedy, Illinois Quilt Research Project, and the Early American Museum, Mahomet, Illinois ("Quilts")

Delinda Chapman ("Voting Rights")

Dr. Don Hallmark, Director, and Richard LaFollette, Frank Lloyd Wright's Dana-Thomas House State Historic Site ("Frank Lloyd Wright")

Bruce Blythe and Rich Newtson ("Exchange")

Kent Western ("Yield")

Lynne and Chuck Sheaff

Marguerite P. Kinkead

John E. Hallwas, William R. Sutton, and Janie Schomberg, manuscript readers for the University of Illinois Press

Deborah Stevenson, Center for Children's Books

*In remembrance of the 844 passengers who drowned
in the Chicago River in 1915 aboard the* Eastland.

Betty Carlson Kay has taught in elementary schools since 1970, mostly in Springfield, Illinois. She is the author of *Jacksonville: The Traditions Continue,* published by Arcadia Press, and five biographies plus a teacher's guide in the children's series Americans of Character, published by Young People's Press. A native of Cicero, Illinois, she now lives in Jacksonville, Illinois, with her husband and enjoys playing the Celtic harp.

Typeset in 15/24 Adobe Garamond
with Berkeley Old Style display
Designed by Copenhaver Cumpston
Composed at the University of Illinois Press
Manufactured by Friesens Corporation

University of Illinois Press
1325 South Oak Street   Champaign, IL 61820-6903
WWW.PRESS.UILLINOIS.EDU